Inq

MW01538602

Faith:

50

Questions

About The

Old

Testament

Answered

TO:

FROM:

DATE:

THIS BOOK BELONGS TO:

_____

_____

_____

_____

_____

_____

_____

_____

INTRODUCTION

Welcome to "Inquisitive Faith: 50 Questions About The Old Testament Answered."

In the vast tapestry of religious literature, the Old Testament stands as a foundational and profound text, rich with history, wisdom, and spiritual insights.

This book embarks on a journey to unravel the mysteries, clarify the uncertainties, and illuminate the wonders that lie within these ancient scriptures in a very simplified way.

As we delve into the heart of the Old Testament, we navigate through 50 carefully selected questions that capture the essence of this sacred text.

INTRODUCTION

Whether you are a seasoned theologian, a curious seeker, or someone exploring your faith, this book serves as a comprehensive guide to understanding the Old Testament in a simple, concise and accessible format.

"Inquisitive Faith" is not just a book; it's an invitation to engage with the Old Testament in a simple and yet very powerful way.

Whether you seek to deepen your faith, broaden your biblical knowledge, or simply satiate your intellectual curiosity, this book is crafted with you in mind.

So, join us on this quest for understanding, where questions are not obstacles but gateways to enlightenment.

INTRODUCTION

"Inquisitive Faith" is an opportunity to explore the profound, challenge the conventional, and embark on a transformative exploration of the Old Testament—a journey that transcends the boundaries of time and speaks to the universal aspects of the human spirit.

WHAT IS THE OLD TESTAMENT?

The Old Testament is the first part of the Bible, comprising books written before the birth of Jesus Christ.

HOW MANY BOOKS ARE IN THE OLD TESTAMENT?

There are 39 books in the Old Testament.

WHAT ARE THE MAIN DIVISIONS IN THE OLD TESTAMENT?

The Old Testament is divided into the Pentateuch, Historical Books, Wisdom Literature, and Prophets.

WHAT IS THE PENTATEUCH?

The Pentateuch, also known as the Torah, consists of the first five books: Genesis, Exodus, Leviticus, Numbers, and Deuteronomy.

5

WHO IS
TRADITIONALLY
BELIEVED TO HAVE
WRITTEN
THE
PENTATEUCH?

Moses is traditionally believed to have written the Pentateuch.

WHAT IS THE BOOK OF GENESIS ABOUT?

Genesis is the book of beginnings, covering the creation, early history, and the patriarchs.

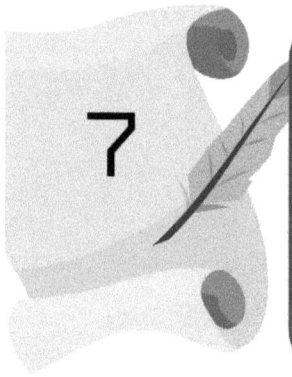

WHAT EVENT
DOES THE BOOK
OF
EXODUS
NARRATE?

Exodus recounts the liberation of the Israelites from slavery in Egypt.

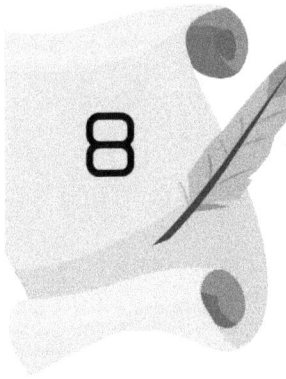

WHAT IS THE CENTRAL THEME OF THE BOOK OF JOSHUA?

Joshua details the Israelites' conquest of the Promised Land.

WHO WAS THE FIRST KING OF ISRAEL ACCORDING TO THE BIBLE?

Saul was the first king of Israel.

WHAT IS THE SIGNIFICANCE OF THE BOOK OF ESTHER?

Esther tells the story of a Jewish queen who saved her people from a plot to destroy them.

WHICH BOOK IS KNOWN FOR ITS EXPLORATION OF THE MEANING OF LIFE?

Ecclesiastes is known for its reflections on the meaning of life.

WHAT IS THE CENTRAL THEME OF THE BOOK OF PROVERBS?

Proverbs imparts practical wisdom for daily living.

WHICH BOOK IS A POETIC DIALOGUE BETWEEN GOD AND A SUFFERING MAN?

The Book of Job is a poetic exploration of human suffering

WHAT IS THE FOCUS OF THE SONG OF SOLOMON?

The Song of Solomon celebrates the beauty of human love and desire.

WHICH BOOK IS TRADITIONALLY ATTRIBUTED TO KING SOLOMON?

Proverbs, Ecclesiastes, and Song of Solomon are traditionally attributed to King Solomon.

16

Isaiah, Jeremiah, Ezekiel, and Daniel are considered Major Prophets.

WHAT IS THE CENTRAL MESSAGE OF THE PROPHET ISAIAH?

Isaiah prophesies about the coming Messiah and God's redemption.

WHAT IS THE BOOK OF JEREMIAH KNOWN FOR?

Jeremiah focuses on God's judgment for disobedience and the promise of restoration.

Ezekiel had a vision of a valley of dry bones in Ezekiel 37.

WHAT IS THE PRIMARY THEME OF THE BOOK OF DANIEL?

Daniel explores the sovereignty of God in the midst of Babylonian exile.

WHAT ARE THE TEN COMMANDMENTS?

The Ten Commandments are moral and ethical principles given by God to Moses on Mount Sinai.

IN WHICH BOOK ARE THE LAWS AND COMMANDMENTS GIVEN TO THE ISRAELITES?

The laws and commandments are primarily found in the Book of Exodus.

WHAT IS THE SIGNIFICANCE OF THE ARK OF THE COVENANT?

The Ark of the Covenant symbolized God's presence among the Israelites.

24

WHAT ARE THE
DIETARY LAWS
MENTIONED IN
THE OLD
TESTAMENT?

The dietary
laws
are
outlined
in Leviticus 11
and
Deuteronomy 14.

WHAT IS THE JUBILEE YEAR, AS MENTIONED IN LEVITICUS?

The Jubilee Year was a special year of liberty and restitution every 50 years.

WHERE IN THE OLD TESTAMENT ARE PROPHECIES ABOUT THE COMING MESSIAH FOUND?

Messianic prophecies are scattered throughout the Old Testament, with significant concentrations in Isaiah, Micah, and Psalms.

WHICH OLD TESTAMENT BOOK PROPHESIES THE VIRGIN BIRTH OF THE MESSIAH?

Isaiah 7:14 prophesies the virgin birth of the Messiah.

IN WHICH TOWN DOES MICAH PREDICT THE MESSIAH WILL BE BORN?

Micah predicts the Messiah's birth in Bethlehem (Micah 5:2).

WHAT IS THE SIGNIFICANCE OF ISAIAH 53 IN MESSIANIC PROPHECY?

Isaiah 53 describes the suffering and atonement of the Messiah.

30

David is often seen as a foreshadowing of the Messiah, especially in Psalms.

WHAT IS THE SIGNIFICANCE OF THE EXODUS EVENT?

The Exodus event symbolizes God's deliverance of the Israelites from slavery.

WHAT IS THE PURPOSE OF THE CONSTRUCTION OF THE TABERNACLE?

The Tabernacle served as a portable sanctuary where God's presence dwelled among the Israelites.

WHAT WAS THE BABYLONIAN CAPTIVITY?

The Babylonian Captivity refers to the period when the Babylonians conquered Judah and exiled the Israelites.

WHAT IS THE STORY OF THE ISRAELITES CROSSING THE JORDAN RIVER?

Joshua led the Israelites in crossing the Jordan River as they entered the Promised Land.

WHO WAS THE QUEEN KNOWN FOR HER BEAUTY AND WISDOM?

Queen Esther is known for her beauty and wisdom.

WHAT ROLE DID DEBORAH PLAY IN THE OLD TESTAMENT?

Deborah was a judge, prophetess, and military leader in ancient Israel.

WHAT IS SOLOMON KNOWN FOR IN THE BIBLE?

Solomon is known for his wisdom, wealth, and the construction of the First Temple in Jerusalem.

WHAT MIRACLE DID GOD PERFORM TO PROVIDE WATER FOR THE ISRAELITES IN THE WILDERNESS?

God made water flow from a rock in the wilderness (Exodus 17:6).

WHAT IS THE STORY OF THE BURNING BUSH IN EXODUS?

God spoke to Moses through a burning bush that was not consumed by the fire (Exodus 3:1-15).

WHAT MIRACULOUS EVENT ALLOWED THE ISRAELITES TO ESCAPE FROM EGYPT?

The parting of the Red Sea allowed the Israelites to escape from Egypt (Exodus 14).

WHAT MIRACLE DID ELISHA PERFORM WITH A WIDOW'S OIL IN 2 KINGS?

Elisha multiplied a widow's oil, allowing her to pay off her debts
(2 Kings 4:1-7).

WHAT SUPERNATURAL EVENT IS ASSOCIATED WITH THE BATTLE OF JERICHO?

The walls of Jericho fell after the Israelites marched around the city and blew trumpets (Joshua 6).

WHO BUILT THE FIRST TEMPLE IN JERUSALEM?

Solomon built the First Temple in Jerusalem.

WHAT WAS THE PURPOSE OF THE DAY OF ATONEMENT IN THE OLD TESTAMENT?

The Day of Atonement was a day of ritual cleansing and reconciliation with God.

WHAT WERE THE ROLES OF THE PRIESTS IN THE OLD TESTAMENT?

Priests were mediators between God and the people, offering sacrifices and performing religious rituals.

46

Major feasts included Passover, Pentecost, Tabernacles, and the Day of Atonement.

WHO WAS THE FIRST JUDGE OF ISRAEL?

Othniel was the first judge of Israel.

WHAT IS THE STORY OF GIDEON AND THE FLEECE?

Gideon asked God for a sign using a fleece, and God granted it twice (Judges 6:36-40).

WHO WAS THE JUDGE AND PROPHETESS KNOWN FOR LEADING ISRAEL IN BATTLE?

Deborah was a judge and prophetess who led Israel in battle against the Canaanites (Judges 4-5).

HOW DID GOD LEAD THE ISRAELITES IN THE WILDERNESS?

God led the Israelites with a pillar of cloud by day and a pillar of fire by night.

Printed in the USA
CPSIA information can be obtained
at www.ICGtesting.com
LVHW061745131223
766431LV00065B/594

9 798880 672776